CONSUMER MATHEMATICS 4
FAMILY FINANCES II

CONTENTS

Author: Barbara Laughman Hintze
Editor-in-Chief: Richard W. Wheeler, M.A.Ed.
Editor: Robin Hintze Kreutzberg, M.B.A.
Consulting Editor: Robert L. Zenor, M.A., M.S.
Illustrator: Thomas R. Rush

Alpha Omega Publications®

804 N. 2nd Ave. E., Rock Rapids, IA 51246-1759
© MCMLXXVIII by Alpha Omega Publications, Inc.   All rights reserved.
LIFEPAC is a registered trademark of Alpha Omega Publications, Inc.

FAMILY FINANCES II

This LIFEPAC® continues the topic of Family Finances that was begun in Consumer Mathematics 3, which presented income, budgets, buying, and taxes. The topics covered in Family Finances II are insurance, banking, and financial planning.

Insurance is a service that helps protect people against financial loss to themselves because of death, illness, fire, flood, or other occurrences. Insurance is also the responsibility of Christian citizens so that bills will not go unpaid in cases of accident, and so that families will not be left penniless in case of death of the family head. This LIFEPAC should encourage you to learn more about your family's insurance.

Banking skills are needed by almost everyone today, and several of the basic skills are taught. The services provided by banks are also included. The LIFEPAC closes with a brief section on financial planning, which is an often neglected but very important part of family finances.

OBJECTIVES

Read these objectives. The objectives tell you what you will be able to do when you have successfully completed this LIFEPAC.

When you have finished this LIFEPAC, you should be able

1. To identify four types of life insurance.

2. To calculate a person's age for insurance purposes.

3. To calculate premiums for varying types and amounts of life insurance.

4. To identify several types of automobile insurance.

5. To calculate premiums for varying types and amounts of automobile insurance.

6. To calculate the amount paid by insurance companies in varying circumstances.

7. To write a check.

8. To keep a record for a checking account.

9. To balance a bank statement.

10. To calculate simple and compound interest on a savings account.

11. To calculate interest on a loan.

12. To list various other services provided by a bank.

13. To calculate the return on shares of stocks, based on declared dividends.

14. To list several ways of disposing of an estate.

Survey the LIFEPAC. Ask yourself some questions about this study. Write your questions here.

_____

_____

_____

_____

_____

_____

_____

_____

_____

_____

_____

_____

_____

I. INSURANCE

OBJECTIVES

1. To identify four types of life insurance.

2. To calculate a person's age for insurance purposes.

3. To calculate premiums for varying types and amounts of life insurance.

4. To identify several types of automobile insurance.

5. To calculate premiums for varying types and amounts of automobile insurance.

6. To calculate the amount paid by insurance companies in varying circumstances.

Insurance is a service furnished by various companies. In essence, you pay the insurance company to protect you against certain events. The insurance company then pays you if the event you are insured against does indeed happen. Several kinds of insurance will be discussed in this section.

~~~~~~~ LIFE INSURANCE ~~~~~~~~~~~~~~~~~~~~~~~

Life insurance might more accurately be called "death insurance." It is insurance against the death of the person holding the policy. When a person holding a life insurance policy dies, certain *benefits* are paid to the survivors named as *beneficiaries*. These benefits depend upon the *face value* of the policy. The persons to whom the benefits are paid thus have a continued source of income, even though the person holding the policy is dead.

NOTE: Examples of insurance premium rates in this LIFEPAC are for practice and calculation purposes. The amounts may not reflect what the student is familar with.

3

DEFINITIONS

A *benefit*, in the sense of insurance, is the amount paid to a survivor upon the death of an insured person.

A *beneficiary* is the survivor to whom the benefits are paid upon the death of an insured person.

The *face value* (also called *face*) of an insurance policy is the stated amount of the policy.

Model: James Harmon takes out an insurance
         policy with a face value of $10,000.
         He names his wife, Nancy, as beneficiary.
         If James should die, Nancy would
         receive $10,000 in benefits.

A person buys life insurance by paying *premiums*. The amount of the premium varies according to four things: (1) the age of the person purchasing the insurance (called the *insured*); (2) the type of insurance policy purchased (four types will be discussed here); (3) the face value of the insurance policy; and (4) whether premiums are paid *annually*, *semiannually*, *quarterly*, or monthly. Also, the cost of insurance sold by one company may be higher or lower than the cost of similar insurance sold by another company.

DEFINITIONS

A *premium* is the amount of money paid for insurance.

Annually means once a year.

Semiannually means twice a year, or every six months.

Quarterly means four times a year, or every three months.

The *insured* is the person purchasing insurance.

Insurance companies set their premiums in such a way that the premiums paid by all of the people they insure will cover the benefits they must pay to the beneficiaries of those who die. This reason is why the premiums are higher for older people: they are more likely to die. Tables of rates that will be fair to the insured and at the same time allow the insurance company to operate without losing money are made up by skilled people who understand statistics. Each insurance company has its own table of rates. The table of TYPICAL LIFE INSURANCE PREMIUMS in Figure 1 in the back of this LIFEPAC is representative and will serve as an example of what rates might be.

Note that the table gives the premium for $1,000 worth of life insurance. This premium must be multiplied by the number of thousands of dollars in the face value of the policy.

Model: The premium listed in the table for a certain kind of insurance is $5.07; $40,000 worth of this kind of insurance would cost 40 x $5.07 or $202.80.

The table of premiums lists four different kinds of insurance. We will discuss each kind.

The least expensive kind of life insurance is *term insurance*. *Term insurance* covers the insured for the stated term of the policy. The term can be one year, five years, ten years, or any other stated period of time. Premiums are paid throughout the term. If the insured dies during the term, the beneficiary receives the face value of the policy. At the end of the term, insurance ceases; and the policy is of no value. The table shows the premiums for term insurance with a term of ten years. Term insurance has no value as

5

an investment, but it provides inexpensive insurance coverage and is
especially useful to the young family
with a limited income but with a great
need for some kind of protection of
wife and children in the event of the
death of the husband and father.

The next kind of insurance, in terms
of expense, is *ordinary whole-life
insurance*. The insured pays premiums
on this type of insurance until his
death. At the time of death, the
face value of the policy is paid to
the beneficiary. In addition, this
type of insurance has a cash value for
the insured if he decides to stop
paying premiums and to cash the
policy in. Thus, ordinary whole-
life insurance has some value as an
investment, although the investment
value is low.

The next most expensive type of
insurance is *limited-payment life
insurance*. This type of insurance
covers the insured for life, but he
only has to pay on it for a certain
number of years. The most usual
limited time is twenty years or thirty
years. A limited-payment life insurance
policy for thirty years, for example, is
called "thirty-payment" or simply "thirty-
pay."

Model: James Harmon takes out $40,000
of twenty-pay life insurance.
He pays premiums on it for twenty
years. At the end of that time,
James no longer has to pay premiums, but the policy remains in
effect until his death, at which
time his beneficiary receives
$40,000.

The most expensive type of insurance
listed in our table is *endowment insurance*.
This type of insurance is insurance with
savings built in. If a person purchases a twenty-year endowment insurance
policy and pays on it for twenty years,

6

at the end of that time, he may collect
the full face value of the policy. That
is to say, if the insured dies before
the policy is paid up, his beneficiary
receives the face of the policy. If
he lives, he himself may collect the
face of the policy. He has, in effect,
purchased insurance *and* endowment.

Note that the table in Figure 1
shows that the amount of the premium
to be paid varies with the age of the
insured. Because women on the whole
have a longer life expectancy than
men, three years are subtracted from
the age of a woman before her age is
looked up in the table. Also note
that for insurance purposes, a person's
age is calculated from his nearest
birthday.

Model: James Harmon was born on March 27,
           1954. On March 27, 1974, he
           celebrated his twentieth birthday.
           For insurance purposes, he is con-
           sidered to be twenty until September
           27, 1974 (six months from his birthday),
           at which time he is nearer twenty-one
           than twenty.

████   Use the table to find the yearly premiums in each of the
         following cases.

1.1   George Anderson takes out $30,000 of twenty-payment life
        insurance. If he is thirty-six years old, what annual
        premium does he pay?

        _____

1.2   Emily Ruth Webster is twenty-seven. (Careful!) She is
        purchasing twenty-year endowment insurance, with a face
        value of $25,000. What is her annual premium?

        _____

1.3   Tom Harris, a young father, is twenty-four years old.
        He wishes to purchase $7,000 of ten-year term insurance.
        What will be his annual premium?

        _____

1.4   Will C. Lowe wishes to purchase an ordinary whole life
       insurance policy with a face value of $50,000. What will
       his annual premium be, if his age for insurance purposes
       is fifty-one?

       _____

█████   In each of the following cases, calculate the age of the
         person for insurance purposes, and then use the chart to
         find the premium he will pay per year for the stated type
         and amount of insurance.

1.5   Clara Sanborn, who was born on July 12, 1936, purchased
       $30,000 worth of ordinary whole-life insurance on
       October 25, 1977. Find

                        a. her age for insurance purposes:

                        _____

                        b. her annual premium:

                        _____

1.6   Bruce Lovegren was born on Septemter 27, 1950. On April
       14, 1977, he purchased a $15,000 ten-year term life
       insurance policy.

                        a. What was his age for insurance
                           purposes?

                        _____

                        b. What was the annual premium he
                           paid?

                        _____

       Insurance companies like for
people to pay their premiums once a
year. When premiums are paid more
frequently, the insurance company
must take care of bookkeeping
expenses. For this reason the cost
to pay premiums semiannually, quarterly,
or monthly is higher. The legend at
the bottom of the table in Figure 1
shows how to find the semiannual,
quarterly, or monthly premium, after
you have found the annual premium.

8

According to this note, semiannual premiums are 51 per cent of the annual premiums; quarterly permiums are 26 per cent of the annual premiums; and monthly premiums are 9 per cent of the annual permiums.

Model: James Harmon is twenty-five when he takes out $40,000 of twenty-pay life insurance. His annual premium is $850.80. If he were to pay semiannual premiums, each premium would be 0.51 x $850.80, or $433.91 Quarterly premiums for this same insurance would be 0.26 x $850.80, or $221.21. Monthly premiums would be 0.09 x $850.80, or $76.57.

▮▮▮▮   Solve the following problems:

1.7   Using the figures from Problem 1.1, what would be the premiums George would pay

   a. semiannually   _____

   b. quarterly   _____

   c. monthly   _____

1.8   Use the figures from Problem 1.5 and find the premiums Clara would pay

   a. semiannually   _____

   b. quarterly   _____

   c. monthly   _____

You should know how much money you would save by paying insurance premiums annually instead of more frequently. The model shows how to figure the difference.

9

Model: James Harmon pays $850.80 per
          year for his life insurance.
          If he were to pay semiannually,
          each premium would be $433.91. His
          total yearly output for premiums would
          be $867.82. The cost for paying the
          premiums semiannually would be
          $867.82 - $850.80 = $17.02.
          If Mr. Harmon were to pay the
          premiums quarterly, the payments would
          be $221.21 each, for a yearly total of
          $884.84. The cost for the privilege of
          quarterly payments would be
          $884.84 - $850.80 = $34.04.
          If he were to pay monthly, the
          payments would be $76.57. The total
          cost would be 12 x $76.57, or $918.84.
          The cost for the privilege of making
          payments monthly would be $68.04.

███ Solve the following problems.

1.9   Using the figures of Problem 1.2, calculate the difference
       between annual and semiannual premiums for Emily Webster.

       _____   _____

1.10   Using the figures of Problem 1.3, calculate the difference
       between annual and quarterly premiums for Tom Harris.

       _____   _____

1.11   Using the figures of Problem 1.4, calculate the difference
       between annual and monthly premiums for Mr. Lowe.

✓ Teacher check_____   _____
                Initial   Date

〰〰〰 **AUTOMOBILE INSURANCE** 〰〰〰〰〰〰〰〰〰〰

    An automobile accident can cause
a great deal of bodily injury and
property damage. The driver who is at
fault in the accident is legally and
morally responsible for the expenses
of such bodily injury and property damage.

Suppose, for example, that you are injured in an accident. If the accident
is not your fault, the person who was
at fault must pay your medical expenses.
On the other hand, if you are at fault
in an accident in which another person
is injured, you must pay all of his
hospital and medical expenses. For
this reason, some sort of automobile
insurance is required by law in every
state. The amount and type required
vary from state to state. Whatever
might be the requirements of your state,
you need to be adequately covered by
automobile insurance. Otherwise, an
accident in which you are at fault
could really hurt your financial
position. Imagine, for example, trying
to pay $20,000 of hospital bills for
a person who was injured in an accident
in which you were at fault. Most
people would not be able to locate
that much money all at once.

Automobile insurance is expensive,
and must be considered as a major
part of the expense of owning and
operating an automobile. Many people
make the mistake of ignoring this
expense, and then find that a car
costs them much more than they had
planned.

To investigate the cost of automobile
insurance, observe the table of AUTOMOBILE
LIABILITY BASIC INSURANCE PREMIUMS in
Figure 2 in the back of this LIFEPAC.
The table lists some typical insurance
premiums for automobile insurance.
First of all, note that the size of the
premium varies according to the *class*.
Class, for automobile insurance purposes,
is determined by age of driver and/or
owner and by the use to which the automobile
is put. This particular table lists
six classes; some insurance companies use
fewer classes and some use more.

Look carefully at the six classes
listed at the bottom of the table.
We shall examine them in detail.

First of all, note that Class 2
is the class that includes male drivers
under twenty-five. Statistics show
that this group of drivers is at fault
in more accidents than any other group;
and, for this reason, the premiums are
higher for this group. Note also that
this group is divided--2A is the class
for drivers under twenty-five who either
do not own the car they drive or who are
married; 2B is the class for drivers
under twenty-five who own their car and
are not married.

Class 3 is an easy one. It includes
all automobiles used primarily for
business purposes. This class is the
one to which "company cars" belong.
However, if any male driver is under
twenty-five, even if the car is used
exclusively for business, the premiums
for Class 2 must be paid.

Class 1 includes all other cars.
Note that the division in Class 1 has
to do with how much the car is used
in transportation to and from work.
If the car is not driven to work, the
insurance is Class 1A. If the car is
driven fewer than ten miles one way to
work, the insurance is Class 1B. Class
1C is for cars driven more than ten miles
to work.

Insurance companies charge different
rates for different people because
different people have different risk
values. As in life insurance, the
automobile insurance company must charge
enough to cover the expenses of the
insurance, and must at the same time
try to be fair to the people paying the
premiums.

Look again at the table of automobile insurance premiums in Figure 2
in the Appendix. Note that two categories
of coverage are listed: bodily injury
and property damage.

Under bodily injury, two figures are
listed for each premium level. The
first of the two figures is the maximum
amount (in thousands of dollars) that
the insurance company will pay for the
expenses of bodily injury to any one
person. The second figure is the maximum total amount (in thousands of
dollars) that the insurance company will
pay for the expenses of bodily injury
in any one accident. For example,
10/20 means that the insurance company
will pay a maximum of $10,000 to any
one person injured in an accident, and
a total maximum of $20,000 for injuries
sustained in one accident.

Model: Suppose John Farmer is at fault
in an accident. In this accident,
Bob Brownlee and his wife and daughter
are injured. Bob's medical expenses
come to $12,000. Mrs. Brownlee's medical
expenses total $8,000. The daughter,
less seriously injured, has a medical
bill of $3,000. If John had insurance
in the amount of 10/20, the insurance
company will pay $10,000 toward Bob's
expenses of $12,000, and $10,000 more
toward the total of $11,000 for the wife
and daughter. John himself is then
responsible for the other $3,000
that the Brownlee family had to pay.
If John had had coverage in the amount
of 50/100, the insurance company would
have covered all of the medical expenses
that resulted from the accident.

In the following cases, determine the amount that the
insurance company will pay. Use Figure 2.

1.12 Sarah Simpson is insured for bodily injury in the amount of
10/20. She is at fault in an accident in which Fred Vail
is injured. Also injured in the accident is a pedestrian,
Arthur Abel. Arthur's medical expenses total $16,000;
Fred's come to $8,000. How much will the insurance pay?

a. _____ for Arthur   c. _____ total

b. _____ for Fred

1.13   Jim Taylor is insured for bodily injury in the amount of
       100/300. He is at fault in an accident in which Marilee
       Medley is injured. Her medical expenses are $40,000.
       How much does the insurance company pay?

_____

     Now look at Figure 2 again and
note the category called *property
damage*. This category includes insurance covering damage that the
insured person does to property belong-
ing to another. Note that premiums are
shown for $5,000; $10,000; and $25,000
worth of property damage insurance.
The figures indicate the maximum
amount that the insurance company will
pay for property damage incurred
in any one accident.

        Model: Daren Smythe was driving his
                  parents' car, with their permission,
                  when he was involved in an accident
                  in which he was at fault. His parents
                  had insurance for property damage with
                  a value of $10,000. In the accident,
                  a car belonging to Henry Willis was
                  damaged, and the cost to repair it was
                  $2,800. Also, a fence on the property
                  of Clarence Forsythe suffered damage.
                  The cost of repairing the fence was
                  $1,500. The insurance company paid all
                  of the expenses involved in this property
                  damage because the total was $4,300, which is
                  less than the $10,000 of coverage.

     Automobile liability insurance
policies usually include bodily injury
and property damage in the same
policy. The amount of insurance is
usually listed with three figures;
for example, 50/100/25. The first two
numbers refer to bodily injury, as explained.
The third figure is the amount (in thousands
of dollars) of the coverage for property
damage.

Now you know enough to be able to figure what the premiums would be on some typical automobile insurance policies.

███████ Calculate the insurance costs.

1.14　a.　What would be the premium for a twenty-one-year-old single man who owns his car, purchasing insurance in the amount of 10/20/5?

_____

　　　　b.　How much would it cost him to purchase insurance in the amount of 100/300/25?

_____

　　　　c.　What is the difference in the cost?

_____

1.15　a.　The Greene family obtains bodily injury and property damage automobile insurance in the amount of 50/100/10. The car that they insure is not driven to work, and no male drivers under twenty-five use the car. What does the Greene family pay as an annual premium?

_____

　　　　b.　When the eldest son in the Greene family becomes seventeen, he is allowed to drive the family car. What is the premium for the Greene family for the same insurance with a seventeen-year-old male driver?

_____

　　　　c.　How much extra do the Greenes pay to insure the seventeen-year-old son?

_____

15

1.16   Wearever Sash Company provides a car for the use of its
        salesmen. They wish to purchase bodily injury and property
        damage insurance in the amount of 100/300/25. If the
        company has no salesmen under twenty-five years old, what
        is their annual premium for this insurance?

        _____

1.17   Randy and Susie Moser are newlyweds. Randy drives their
        car to his job, twenty-seven miles away from home, each
        day. If Randy and Susie are both twenty, what premiums
        would they pay for bodily injury and property damage
        insurance in the amount of 50/100/10?

        _____

    So far, we have only discussed in-
surance that pays for bodily injury
and property damage of someone other
than the insured. Suppose, however,
that a young person accidentally hits
a lightpost, and injures himself and
does some damage to his car. Some types
of automobile insurance will pay his
expenses in such a case. The youth's
medical expenses would be paid if he
had insurance called automobile *medical
payments insurance*. The table of ANNUAL
PREMIUMS FOR AUTOMOBILE MEDICAL PAYMENTS
in Figure 3 in the back of this LIFEPAC
shows typical costs for such medical
insurance.

        Model: Jim Carver runs his car into a ditch.
                        In the accident, Jim breaks a leg.
                        He has medical payments insurance
                        in the amount of $500. Since Jim
                        is a driver in Class 1A, this in-
                        surance costs him $20 a year. Jim's
                        medical expenses, including a day
                        in the hospital, came to $375.
                        His insurance pays the total bill.

    Damage to the automobile of the
insured person is covered under insurance called *collision insurance*.
This insurance is usually sold with
a deductible clause. That is, the

insured pays the first $50 or $100
or whatever the deductible amount is;
and the insurance pays the rest.

Model: Richard is involved in an
          accident in which $1,250 worth
          of damage is done to his car.
          He is at fault in the accident.
          He is insured for collision,
          with a $100-deductible clause.
          Richard must pay the first $100
          of the repair bill, but the in-
          surance company pays the rest.
          Note that if the damage to Richard's
          car had been less than $100, the
          insurance company would not have
          paid anything, since Richard has
          a $100 deductible policy.

The premiums for collision insurance vary
with the amount of the deductible clause and
the age and size of the car. Newer, bigger
cars have bigger premiums, because the costs
to repair them are greater. Refer to the
table of ANNUAL AUTOMOBILE COLLISION INSURANCE
RATES in Figure 4 in the back of this LIFEPAC.
Notice that cars are divided into three size
groups and three age groups. The class of
the driver and the car usage must also be
taken into consideration.

Model: $100-deductible
          collision insurance for
          a compact car in Class
          3 that is four years
          old can be purchased
          for a premium of $56
          per year, according to
          the chart.

From the table in Figure 4, find the premiums for collision insurance in each of the following cases.

1.18   A $50-deductible insurance policy for a luxury car of the current year, with a driver in Class 3

                        Annual premium: _____

1.19   A $100-deductible insurance policy for a full-size car of last year, with a driver in Class 2A

                        Annual premium: _____

1.20   A $100-deductible insurance policy for a compact car of year before last, with a driver in Class 1

                        Annual premium: _____

Calculate how much the insurance company would pay in benefits in each of the following cases.

1.21   Sam has purchased collision insurance with a $100-deductible clause, and automobile medical payments insurance in the amount of $500. In an accident in which Sam is at fault, Sam incurs injuries for a total expense of $650. Also, $1,400 worth of damage is done to Sam's car. How much does the insurance company pay Sam?

                        _____

1.22   Glenda has automobile insurance with medical payments in the amount of $2,000, and $50-deductible collision insurance. In an accident in which Glenda is at fault, $350 worth of damage is done to her car. In addition, Glenda spends a day at the hospital for observation. (She is found to have no serious injuries and released, but her hospital bill is $276.) How much will the insurance company pay for Glenda's expenses?

                        _____

We should discuss one more kind of automobile insurance in this section. It is called *comprehensive insurance*. This insurance pays for damage to an automobile caused by such things as weather, theft, and vandalism. Comprehensive policies can be sold with a deductible clause, which makes them much cheaper to buy. Also, many comprehensive policies have clauses excluding high-risk automobile accessories, such as stereos and tape decks.

As shown by the table of ANNUAL AUTOMOBILE
COMPREHENSIVE INSURANCE RATES in Figure 5,
in the back of this LIFEPAC, premiums for
comprehensive insurance are affected by
the age and size of the car. The class
of the driver does not affect comprehensive
insurance.

Model: William pays $32 per year for
             comprehensive coverage of his new
             full-size car. When a hailstorm
             caused $250 worth of damage to the
             paint on the car, the insurance
             company paid for repairing the
             damage.

█████   From the table in Figure 5, find the premiums for the
         following comprehensive insurance policies.

1.23   A comprehensive policy for a full-size, five-year-old car

_____

1.24   A policy covering a luxury car that is one year old

_____

1.25   A comprehensive policy for a new compact car

_____

    Many insurance companies offer what
they call "good driver discounts." If
an insured person drives for three years
without having a driving accident, the
company reduces his rate to 90 per
cent of what it would otherwise be. On
the other hand, if the driver has several
accidents within one year, the insurance
company will likely increase his rates.
Typically, one accident will cause the
premiums to be 110 per cent of what they
would otherwise be; two accidents will
cause the rate to be 150 per cent of
a normal rate; three accidents, 200 per
cent; and four accidents within a year,
250 per cent. More than four accidents
within one year may result in cancellation
of the automobile insurance policy.

19

Model: Noel's basic auto insurance premium totals $314.00. After three years with no accidents, Noel's premium is reduced to 90 per cent of $314, or $282.60. Then, Noel has three accidents within one year. The next year, her insurance premium is 200 per cent of $314.00, or $628.

Since comprehensive insurance is not based on the class of the driver, it is not affected by accidents. Therefore, the rate for comprehensive insurance is not subject to reduction for good drivers or to increase for bad drivers.

Calculate the premiums for the following insurance policies.

1.26 Dick's basic insurance cost is $613.50 per year. His insurance company offers a typical "safe-driver discount." What would be his rate if he went three years without an accident?

_____

1.27 Mary pays $417.25 for automobile insurance, of which $32 is for comprehensive coverage. One year, Mary has two accidents. What will her premium be the next year? (Careful: Subtract the $32 before you take 150 per cent, then add it back in to get the total!)

_____

1.28 In the table in Figure 2, find the premium for 10/20/10 insurance for a driver in Class 2A. Then calculate what the premium would be the year after this driver has four accidents.

_____

 Teacher check_____
                              Initial   Date

20

Insurance companies sell many other types of insurance. In fact, you can buy insurance for almost anything, if you are willing to shop and to pay for the insurance. Some of the more common types of miscellaneous insurance are discussed and explained here.

Homeowners' insurance protects against a loss of home and furnishings caused by fire, theft, or natural disaster. When a person purchases such insurance on the contents of his home, he is often required to make a careful inventory of the things he owns so that the insurance company is not responsible for imaginary or false claims. Homeowners' insurance covers an interesting variety of losses. One teen-ager borrowed an expensive musical instrument from his high school. The musical instrument fell out of the pick-up truck in which it was being transported and was severely damaged. The repair bill was $175. The homeowners' insurance policy held by the teen-ager's mother covered the loss, and the insurance company paid the bill.

Liability insurance protects a person against injury to other people on his property. For example, if someone slips on your sidewalk, liability insurance will often pay his medical expenses. This kind of insurance is often purchased by institutions to protect them against lawsuits from people injured on their property.

Fire insurance is often included in a homeowners' policy, but it can be purchased separately also. This type of insurance pays for damages

21

caused by fire. It is often purchased by factories and corporations. Fire insurance can be purchased to cover a building, or the contents of the building, or both.

Hospitalization insurance pays for hospital care. Because of the high and rising cost of hospitalization in our country, many people believe that everybody should be covered by some kind of hospitalization insurance. Most hospitalization policies are part of a group plan, usually purchased through the company where one works, the school one attends, or perhaps the credit union where one does business. Each hospitalization policy is different, with different premiums and different provisions for maximum benefits, maximum stay in the hospital, maximum amounts for specific kinds of procedures, and so on.

Some group hospitalization plans are also medical payment plans. These plans pay not only hospital expenses but also all or part of ordinary doctor bills. Some such plans also include dental benefits. A careful reading of each individual policy is the only way to be sure exactly what is, or is not, covered by the policy.

In our country we have a type of medical insurance provided by the government for the elderly and others called Medicare. The costs of this insurance plan are paid partly by the workers in our country through their Social Security taxes and partly by the Federal Government.

Miscellaneous types of insurance are many. Most doctors and lawyers carry malpractice insurance that protects them against lawsuits for *malpractice*, which means not performing the job to the satisfaction of the client. Temporary insurance can be purchased to cover, for example,

a church picnic or an airplane trip.
Insurance can be purchased to cover the
loss of any particularly valuable item.
A corporation might purchase insurance
against the death or disability of the
corporation president. In fact, as
already mentioned, if you will shop for
it, and can pay for it, you can buy
insurance to cover almost anything.

███ Match the type of insurance to the coverage it provides.

1.29 _____ automobile

1.30 _____ homeowners'

1.31 _____ hospitalization

1.32 _____ fire

1.33 _____ liability

1.34 _____ malpractice

1.35 _____ life

a. protects against loss from death
   of insured

b. protects against loss from injury
   to others on insured's property

c. protects against loss from hospital
   expenses to insured

d. protects against loss from automobile accidents of insured

e. protects against loss from lawsuits against insured

f. protects against loss to insured's
   home and furnishings

g. protects against loss from insured's being dismissed from his
   job

h. protects against loss from fire
   on insured's property

███ Write *true* or *false*.

1.36 _____ Endowment life insurance is the least expensive
             type of life insurance to purchase.

1.37 _____ Comprehensive auto insurance is not based on the
             insurance class of the driver.

1.38 _____ Male drivers under the age of 25 have been found to be at fault in more accidents than any other group of people.

1.39 _____ An insurance policy with terms of 10/20/5 means that the insurance company will pay medical expenses for 10 out of 20 people injured and 5 out of 20 people hospitalized.

1.40 _____ Term insurance provides inexpensive life insurance with no savings feature.

■ (OPTIONAL) Complete this exercise.

1.41 Find out all the kinds of insurance that your family has. Talk with your parents about why they have the kinds of insurance they have. Make a list of some ways your family could improve its insurance plans.

✓ **Teacher check** _____
　　　　　　　 Initial 　 Date

 Review the material in this section in preparation for the Self Test. The Self Test will check your mastery of this particular section. The items missed on this Self Test will indicate specific areas where restudy is needed for mastery.

SELF TEST 1

(Students will need access to all of the tables in this section to complete Self Test 1.)

Write the name of the correct type of insurance on each blank (each answer, 2 points).

term   limited-payment life

ordinary whole life   endowment

1.01   Insurance that covers the insured for life, for which he

        only has to pay a certain number of years, is _____.

1.02   Insurance that covers the insured only for a specific, stated

        term, such as 10 years, is _____.

1.03   Insurance that covers the insured for life, and for which

        premiums are paid by the insured until his death, is

        _____.

1.04   Insurance that provides both insurance and savings is

        _____.

Use the table in Figure 1 to find the premiums in each of the following cases (each answer, 3 points).

1.05   Simon Simms takes out $10,000 of twenty-payment life when
        he is nineteen years old.

                            a. annual premium _____

                            b. quarterly premium

                            _____

1.06   Richard Henry takes out $25,000 of ordinary whole life when
        he is forty-three years old.

                            a. annual premium _____

                            b. semiannual premium

                            _____

1.07   Marice Ann Webber, twenty-five, takes out $15,000 of term
        insurance for a 10-year term.

                                a. annual premium _____

                                b. monthly premium _____

1.08   Sharon Bradson takes out a $12,000 endowment insurance
        policy when she is thirty-seven years old.

                                a. annual premium _____

                                b. quarterly premium

                                                   _____

Calculate the age of the following people for insurance purposes
on the given date (each answer, 3 points).

1.09   Hannah Wright, who was born October 12, 1953, is how old
        (for insurance purposes) on April 1, 1978?

                                                   _____

1.010   William Wallace, born December 28, 1934, is how old
        (for insurance purposes) on June 2, 1978?

                                                   _____

Solve the following problems related to automobile insurance (each
answer, 3 points).

1.011   What would be the premium for Harold White, a nineteen-year-
        old, single man who owns his car and who purchases bodily
        injury and property damage car insurance in the amount
        of 50/100/10?

                                                   _____

1.012   If Harold White (see Problem 1.011) is at fault in an
        accident in which Bill Bland and his wife and daughter
        are injured, how much will the insurance company pay
        if costs of medical care are as shown?

                Bill Bland $ 8,000

                Mrs. Bland $65,000

                Bland's daughter $20,000

                                                   _____

1.013 If the insurance company does not pay the total amount in Problem 1.012, who must pay for it?

_____

1.014 What is the premium for $50-deductible collision insurance for a compact car of the current year, with a driver in Class 1?

_____

1.015 If Jerry Adams would normally pay $875 for bodily injury and property damage insurance, find his premium for the year after he has three accidents.

_____

Complete this list (each answer, 3 points).

1.016 List at least five kinds of insurance that one can buy.

a. _____

b. _____

c. _____

d. _____

e. _____

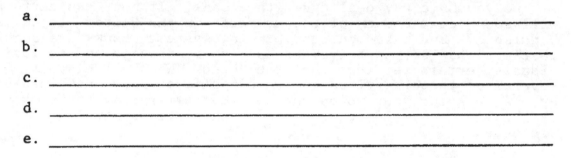

$\boxed{\begin{array}{c} 54 \\ \diagdown \\ 68 \end{array}}$

Score _____

Teacher check _____

Initial   Date

27

II. BANKING

Do you have any dealings with a bank? If not, you certainly will soon because much of the commerce in the United States is handled by, and based on, the banking system. Banks are service institutions, set up to render both to businesses and to individuals certain services that they need. We shall discuss several of these services in two classifications: services offered by the bank for your money and services offered by the bank using the bank's money. Other types of bank services will also be presented.

YOUR MONEY

Banks are regulated by law. Placing your money in a bank requires that you open an account. There are many different types of accounts. However, two of the most common services for your money offered by banks involve either checking accounts or savings accounts. Savings accounts and some checking accounts enable you to earn interest for money you place, or deposit, in the bank. A checking account allows you to write an instruction to the bank, as a check, to make a payment from that account. Electronic payments can also be made from many checking accounts with a debit card. Debit cards can also be known as bank cards, check cards, or cash cards.

Whether you have a checking account or a savings account each time you make a deposit the bank will add to your balance. The bank will usually have savings deposit slips for you to use. Each time you make a withdrawal the bank will deduct the money from your account.

CHECKING ACCOUNTS
A checking account operates very simply. You deposit your money in the bank. When you wish to use some of your money, you write a check. This check tells the bank to take money from your account and pay it to the person who holds

the check. A debit card functions in a similar way but the electronic transfer from your account to the account of the other person or business takes place immediately. The bank keeps track of how much money you have left in your account and sends you a statement each month or makes the information available online. A charge is usually made for this service. However, some banks offer free checking accounts, and others do not charge if the minimum balance in the account does not fall below a certain amount.

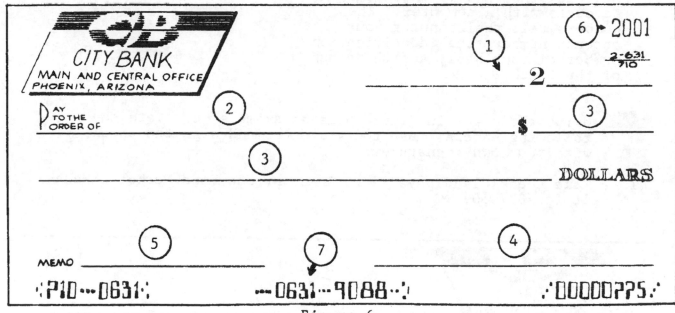

Figure 6

Figure 6 shows a typical check. Note several features of the check.

1   The check has a place for the date to be written in.

2   The words "Pay to the order of" are followed by a blank, on which is written the name of the person or firm to whom the check is to be paid.

3   The amount of the check is written in numbers on one blank and in words on another blank. This duplication is to prevent anyone from changing the amount of the check.

4   The check has a place for your signature. The check is not valid unless it is signed by the owner of the account.

5   The check has a place to write in any
     memos or comments, such as your bill
     number or the purpose of the check.

6   The check is numbered so that you
     can keep track of it.

7   Some oddly-shaped numbers are along
     the bottom of the check. These numbers
     are to be read by a computer.
     All banks now handle checking
     accounts with a computer. The
     numbers tell the computer your
     account number, the identification
     number of your bank, and the amount
     of the check.

█████ Using the check in Figure 6 as an example, complete the
       following checks. Use today's date, and sign the checks
       with your own signature.

2.1   Make check #1456 payable to Grand Avenue Food Market. Make
       it for $37.50.

CITY BANK
MAIN AND CENTRAL OFFICE
PHOENIX, ARIZONA

1456

2-631
710

2

PAY
TO THE
ORDER OF $

                                                      DOLLARS

MEMO _____

⑆710⋯0631⑆   ⋯0631⋯9088⑈   ⑈00003750⑈

2.2 Make check #1457 payable to Glendale Community Church. Make it for $47.98. In the memo, write "tithe."

```
                                                                    1457
    CITY BANK                                                        2-631
    MAIN AND CENTRAL OFFICE                         2                 710
    PHOENIX, ARIZONA

    PAY
    TO THE
    ORDER OF                                           $

                                                            DOLLARS

    MEMO _____           _____

    ⑆710⋯0631⑆        ⋯0631⋯9088⋯⑈        ⑈00004798⑈
```

Every time you write a check, you must record how much money you have left in your account so that you will not overdraw your account. To write a check that you do not have money in the bank to cover is illegal. For this reason you must keep careful records of the checks you write. Your bank will provide you with a record book. When you make a deposit, you write it in your record book and *add* the amount to your account. When you write a check, you write it in your record book and *subtract* it from your account. A typical record book is shown in Figure 7.

CHECK NO	DATE	CHECKS ISSUED TO OR DESCRIPTION OF DEPOSIT	AMOUNT OF CHECK		AMOUNT OF DEPOSIT		BALANCE FORWARD	
							6 75	32
1042	12/18	To Lucky's For food	73	24			Check or Dep. 73	24
							Bal. 602	08
	12/20	To DEPOSIT For PAYCHECK			434	00	Check or Dep. 434	00
							Bal. 1036	08
1043	12/22	To Kinney's For shoes	27	58			Check or Dep. 27	58
							Bal. 1008	50
		To For					Check or Dep.	
							Bal.	
		To For					Check or Dep.	
							Bal.	
		To For					Check or Dep.	
							Bal.	

Figure 7

31

On the following checking account record, enter the figures and add or subtract them to keep the running total correct.

2.3 The balance forward is $358.27.

    a. Check #3427 for $23.42 to Adam's Meat Market for food

    b. Check #3428 for $14.95 to West High School for books and supplies

    c. Deposit of $276.50, a paycheck

    d. Check #3429 for $219.93 to Saguaro Mortgage Company for house payment

    e. Check #3430 for $76.84 to Alamo Power and Light for last month's electricity

CHECK NO.	DATE	CHECKS ISSUED TO OR DESCRIPTION OF DEPOSIT	AMOUNT OF CHECK		AMOUNT OF DEPOSIT		BALANCE FORWARD	
		To					Check or Dep	
		For					Bal	
		To					Check or Dep	
		For					Bal	
		To					Check or Dep	
		For					Bal	
		To					Check or Dep	
		For					Bal	
		To					Check or Dep	
		For					Bal	
		To					Check or Dep	
		For					Bal	

At the end of each month, the bank sends you a statement of the activity in your checking account. The bank also sends you all of the checks that they have paid for you during the month. These checks are marked *PAID*, and are called *cancelled* checks. You should always save all your cancelled checks, because they can serve as proof of payment if a question ever arises about whether you have paid a certain bill.

CONSUMER MATHEMATICS
4

LIFEPAC TEST

Name _____

Date _____

Score _____

CONSUMER MATHEMATICS 4: LIFEPAC TEST

(Students will need access to all tables in this LIFEPAC to complete the LIFEPAC Test.)

Match the type of insurance to its definition (each answer, 2 points

1. _____ ordinary whole life

2. _____ collision auto

3. _____ term life

4. _____ medical payment auto

5. _____ property damage auto

6. _____ endowment life

7. _____ comprehensive auto

8. _____ bodily injury auto

9. _____ limited-payment life

a. covers insured for a specific term

b. covers insured for life; is paid for life

c. covers insured for life; is paid on for a specific number of years

d. provides life insurance and savings

e. pays if insured is at fault and insured is hurt

f. pays if insured is at fault and someone else is hurt

g. pays if insured is at fault and someone else's property is damaged

h. pays if insured is at fault and his own car is damaged

i. pays if car is stolen

Complete these items (each answer, 3 points)

10. Emily Webster is 27. (Remember that adjustments are made to women's ages for insurance purposes.) She is purchasing a 20-year endowment insurance, with a face value of $25.000. What is her annual premium?

11. Bruce Lovegren was born on September 27, 1950. On April 14, 1977, he purchased a $15,000 10-year term life insurance policy.

a. What was his age for insurance purposes?

b. What was the annual premium he paid?

12. a. What would be the premium for a 21-year-old, single man who owns his car, purchasing insurance in the amount of 10/20/5?

_____

   b. How much would it cost him to purchase insurance in the amount to 100/300/25?

_____

   c. What is the difference in the cost?

_____

13. What is the annual premium for $100-deductible insurance for a full-size car of last year, with a driver in Class 2A?

_____

14. Jim Taylor is insured for bodily injury in the amount of 100/300. He is at fault in an accident in which Marilee Medley is injured. Her medical expenses are $40,000. How much does the insurance company pay?

_____

15. Use the following figures to find out if an error exists in either the bank's balance or the customer's record book.

   The ending balance on the statement is $378.19. Three checks are outstanding: #5104 for $30.90; #5123 for $17.50; and #5124 for $98.10. A deposit of $309.00 has not yet been credited. A service charge of $4.21 has been made. The balance in the record book is $544.90. Does an error exist?

_____

16. Find the total amount and the amount of interest earned on $6,500 at 6% for 25 years.

	TOTAL AMOUNT	INTEREST AMOUNT
compounded annually	a._____	b._____
compounded semiannually	a._____	b._____
compounded quarterly	a._____	b._____

17.   MS&T has 100,000 share of stock outstanding.

   a. If it declares dividends of $50,000, what is the
      dividend per share? _____

   b. Marty owns 25 shares of stock in MS&T. What is his
      share of this declared dividend? _____

Write the following list (each item, 3 points).

18.   List four ways a person can dispose of his estate.

   a. _____
      _____

   b. _____
      _____

   c. _____
      _____

   d. _____
      _____

When you get your bank statement, you should check it to see if you and the bank agree as to how much money you have. If not, you need to find the error. If the error is in the figures in your record book, you must correct the figures so that you will not overdraw. If the error is on the part of the bank, you must notify them within ten days from the receipt of the statement. Otherwise, the bank will assume that the statement is correct.

The following steps should be used to balance a bank statement.

1. Arrange all of the cancelled checks in numerical order. Note the ones that are missing. These checks are called *outstanding checks*. They are checks that you have written, but that have not yet arrived at the bank to be subtracted from your account. Make a list of these outstanding checks, with the amounts for which they were written. Add these amounts.

2. On the bank statement, find the amount called "ending balance." This amount is the balance the bank has credited you with at the end of the statement period. Subtract from that balance the total amount of the outstanding checks.

3. In your record book, look at the very latest entry. Check to be sure that all deposits included in your record book are included on the bank statement. If you have added a deposit that the bank has not added, add it now to the amount in Step 2.

4. Check the bank statement to see if any service charges or other charges have been subtracted from your account. If so, enter them in your record book and subtract them from your balance.

5. If the record has no errors, the amount you got in Step 2 (or Step 3 if you added a deposit) on the bank's statement should be exactly the same as the amount you got in Step 4 in your record book. If the amounts do not agree, you must make a more extensive check to locate the error. Sometimes you might need to seek the assistance of an accounts clerk or bookkeeper at the bank. Generally, bank employees are willing and able to help you find the reasons for any problem you might have in checking your statement.

▉▉▉ Using the following information, check to see if either the bank statement or the customer's record book appear to have any errors.

2.4 The ending balance on the statement is $637.89. Three checks are outstanding: #4577 for $25.00; #4593 for $75.21; and #4599 for $117.84. A deposit of $216.00 has not yet been credited to the account. A service charge of $4.19 has been made. The balance in the record book is $640.03. Does an error exist?

_____

2.5 The ending balance on the statement is $1,227.75. Two checks are outstanding, #345 for $200.00 and #421 for $7.16. No deposits are unrecorded and no service charge is made. The balance in the record book is $1,027.75. Does an error exist?

_____

Complete this activity.

2.6 List the five steps to be followed in balancing a bank statement.

a. _____

_____

_____

b. _____

_____

_____

c. _____

_____

_____

d. _____

_____

_____

e. _____

_____

_____

SAVINGS ACCOUNTS

The other main service that banks offer for your money is a savings account. If you use this service, you deposit money in the bank to earn *interest* rather than to write checks. The bank pays you interest on money that you keep in a savings account. The amount of interest depends on the going rate of interest in the country as a whole, the length of time the

money is left in the bank, and other
factors, depending on each individual
bank. The two basic kinds of interest
are *simple interest* and *compound interest*.
In *simple interest* the bank pays
certain per cent of the amount in the
savings account at set intervals, usually
yearly. Most savings accounts, however,
earn *compound interest*. Simply explained,
an account that earns compound interest
earns interest not only on the original
amount but also on the interest
already paid. Interest can be compounded
annually, semiannually, or monthly. Some
banks and savings institutions compound
interest daily. With the help of com-
puters, interest can be compounded
"continually," which means that, in
effect, a savings account is growing
constantly.

DEFINITIONS

Interest is the money paid by banks on money in savings accounts.

Simple interest is interest figured only on the amount of money
in the savings account.

Compound interest is interest figured on the amount of money
in the savings account plus the amount of interest already
earned.

Simple interest is easy to figure.
The formula for simple interest is
$I = P$ x R x T. I represents interest.
P represents principal, which refers
to the amount in the account. R
stands for rate of interest, expressed
as a certain per cent of the money on
deposit. T represents time, and since
the rate of interest is usually
expressed in a certain per cent per
year, time is considered in years.

Model 1: The simple interest earned on a
deposit of $3,000 at 6% for 5 years
is $3,000 x 0.06 x 5 = $900.
(Remember to change 6% to 0.06.)

For the purposes of banks' interest,
the year is considered to have 360 days.
If interest is paid for a certain number
of days, that number of days is divided
by 360 to express the time in years.

Model 2:   The simple interest earned on a
deposit of $4,000 at 5% for 120
days is $4,000 x 0.05 x $\frac{120}{360}$ =
= $4,000 x 0.05 x 0.33 = $66.67.

████   Compute the amount of interest earned in the following
simple interest problems.

2.7   A deposit of $800 at 3.5% for 7 years

_____

2.8   A deposit of $1,600 at 6% for 180 days

_____

2.9   A deposit of $100 at 8% for 20 years

_____

2.10   A deposit of $4,500 at 5% for 3 years

_____

2.11   A deposit of $10,000 at 9.5% for 90 days

_____

2.12   A deposit of $295 at 7% for 270 days

_____

2.13 A deposit of $500 at 4.8% for 5 years

_____

2.14 A deposit of $3,000 at 10% for 1 year

_____

Compound interest is not so easy to figure. In fact, the best way to figure compound interest is to use a table. ' The table of the AMOUNT OF $1 AT COMPOUND INTEREST in Figure 8 in the back of this LIFEPAC shows the amount to which $1.00 grows after certain periods at several different rates of interest. This figure differs from the interest earned amount you figured in the last set of exercises because this figure includes the principal plus the interest, not just the interest. If the interest is compounded annually, you read the table directly.

Model: To find the amount that results when $4,000 is compounded at 6% annually over seven years, find in the chart the amount of $1.00 at 6% for seven years and multiply by $4,000: 1.5036303 x 4,000 = $6,014.52. To find out how much of that figure is interest, subtract the original investment: $6,014.52 - $4,000 = $2,014.52. The $4,000 earned $2,014.52 in interest over seven years.

▉ Find the total amount and amount of interest earned in the following compound interest problems.

                    TOTAL AMOUNT   INTEREST AMOUNT

2.15 $650 at 8% for 14 years, compounded annually

                    a._____   b._____

38

2.16 $1,050 at 6% for 25 years, compounded annually

a._____   b._____

2.17 $5,000 at 3% for 10 years, compounded annually

a._____   b._____

2.18 $500 at 4% for 5 years, compounded annually

a._____   b._____

2.19 $2,900 at 1.5% for 3 years, compounded annually

a._____   b._____

2.20 $850 at 2% for 9 years, compounded annually

a._____   b._____

Because of the way the chart is set up, we must adjust the way we read it if the interest is compounded semiannually or quarterly. Follow this rule: If the interest is compounded semiannually, look up on the chart *half* the rate and *twice* the years. If the interest is compounded quarterly, look up *one-fourth* the rate and *four times* the years.

Model 1:   To find the amount to which $5,000 would grow in ten years at 6% compounded semiannually, look up $1.00 at 3% for twenty years and multiply by $5,000. According to the chart $1.00 at 3% for twenty years is 1.8061112. When you multiply that number by $5,000 you get $9,033.56.

Model 2:   To find the amount to which $5,000 would grow in ten years at 6% compounded quarterly, look up $1.00 at 1½% for forty years. According to the chart, $1.00 at 1½% for forty years is 1.8140184. Multiplied by $5,000, the answer is $9,070.92. Note that compounding quarterly yields a higher interest amount than compounding semiannually.

Find the total amount and amount of interest paid in the following compound interest problems.

		TOTAL AMOUNT	INTEREST AMOUNT
2.21	$3,000 at 8% for 5 years		
	compounded annually	a._____	b._____
	compounded semiannually	c._____	d._____
	compounded quarterly	e._____	f._____
2.22	$900 at 6% for 10 years		
	compounded annually	a._____	b._____
	compounded semiannually	c._____	d._____
	compounded quarterly	e._____	f._____
2.23	$5,000 at 8% for 2 years		
	compounded annually	a._____	b._____
	compounded semiannually	c._____	d._____
	compounded quarterly	e._____	f._____
2.24	$1,500 at 6% for 25 years		
	compounded annually	a._____	b._____
	compounded semiannually	c._____	d._____
	compounded quarterly	e._____	f._____

Teacher check_____
                Initial   Date

〜〜〜〜〜THEIR MONEY 〜〜〜〜〜

So far, we have been talking about the services of a bank that have to do with your money and the way the bank helps you take care of it. Banks also provide services that involve the bank's money. Two of these most common services are lending money and providing credit cards.

LOANS

If you have a steady job and a good record of paying your bills, the bank will usually lend you money for a good reason. Some common reasons for borrowing money are to buy a car, to buy a home, to make improvements on a home, to pay a sudden large expense such as a hospital bill, to pay for the college education of a child, and other similar causes. When you borrow money, you must pay for the use of it. The money you pay is called *interest*. You should be able to see that, when the bank pays you interest for the use of your money in a savings account and when you pay the bank for the use of their money in a loan, the same concept is being applied. Again, the formula for interest is $I = P \times R \times T$, where I is the interest; P is the principal, or amount borrowed; R is the rate of interest; and T is the time of the loan.

Model: The interest to be paid on a loan of $500 at 12% for 4 years is $500 x 0.12 x 4 = $240. The total amount that will be owed to the bank at the end of four years is $240 + $500 = $740.

Solve these problems.

2.25 Find the interest due on $250 at 11% for 2 years.

_____

2.26 Find the interest due on $1,400 at 9% for 270 days (remember that for bank interest purposes, a year is considered to have 360 days.)

_____

41

2.27   Find the interest due on $5,000 at 11% for 3 years.

_____

2.28   Find the interest due on $700 at 10.5% for 90 days.

_____

2.29   Find the interest due on $1,090 at 8% for 5 years.

_____

CREDIT CARDS
    Bank credit cards have come to be
an important factor in the economy of
the United States. Many people find
that they cannot do business without
a credit card. Many places of
business will not take a check from
a person who does not have a major
credit card to guarantee payment of
the check. In addition, many people
find that a credit card helps them
keep track of their expenditures.
    A credit card works in the follow-
ing fashion. When you buy something
and "put it on your credit card,"
you are (in effect) asking the bank
to pay for the item for you. Then,
at the end of the month, the bank
sends you a list of the things that
it has paid for, at your direction,
and you pay the bank. In most cases,
if you pay the total amount that
you have charged to your credit card
within the month, the bank does not
charge you anything for this service.
On the other hand, if you do not pay
the entire bill, you are charged
interest on the unpaid part, because
this amount really is a loan that the
bank has made to you to purchase the
items you "put on your credit card."
One true advantage of credit-card
buying is the monthly list you receive

of your expenditures. Such a list can
be very helpful at tax time to find
items for which you are entitled to
tax deductions. Also, such a list is
helpful in managing your personal
budget.

On the other hand, real dangers
exist in the undisciplined use of
credit cards. Because of the ease of
"putting it on the credit card,"
many people buy things they do not need
and cannot actually afford. When the
bill comes, they cannot pay the total
amount. This process sometimes continues
until the family finds itself in financial
trouble, very deeply in debt. Be careful
in your use of credit cards. Be sure
that you control their use, rather than
letting credit buying control you.

■■■■■ Write *true* or *false*.

2.30 _____ When you purchase an item with a credit card, you
might not ever have to pay for it.

2.31 _____ Actually, buying with a credit card involves getting
a loan from the bank.

2.32 _____ One advantage of credit-card buying is the monthly
list of expenditures you receive.

2.33 _____ Buying with credit cards causes no major problems.

2.34 _____ Credit cards do not form a very important part
of the economy of the United States.

~~~~~~~OTHER SERVICES ~~~~~~~~~~~~~~~~

Besides savings and checking accounts, banks offer other
financial services. A bank can provide you with financial counseling relating to investments, wills, estate
planning, and the like. These services are usually
available to bank customers free or for a minimal fee.

You can rent a safety deposit box in the bank's vault,
usually for a fee. This service provides a safe, protected place to keep important papers, valuable docu-
ments, and even valuable jewelry. The box is private;
only you can open it. It is protected from fire and
theft. Items stored therein do not get lost. This
service is important to many people.

From a bank you can obtain a cashier's check or a cer-
tified check. These checks are items that will be
accepted even when your personal check will not, because
they are guaranteed by the bank itself, not just by
your signature. Usually a small charge is made for such
a check.

From a bank you can obtain traveler's checks. These checks are highly acceptable, easily cashed checks that you can use in places even when you are not known. A standard fee is charged for every hundred dollars' worth of-traveler's checks purchased. Traveler's checks can often be replaced if they are lost or stolen, and for this reason they are safer to carry than cash. Many people use them when they go on trips. Also, a bank can provide currency exchange. In other words, if you are going to a foreign country, a bank can sell you money of that country in exchange for dollars.

ATM'S

Many banks offer a variety of electronic banking features. The most familiar may be the Automated Teller Machine or ATM.

A customer is issued a card by his bank and a Personal Identification Number or PIN. This permits the customer to make deposits and withdrawals whether the bank is open or not by using a special computer terminal.

This service is helpful for people on special schedules. You can access cash at an airport or in a distant city just by using the card. Merchants, like supermarkets, are often equipped for these debit transactions.

There can be disadvantages to using ATM's. For example, withdrawals may have to be in certain size bills. It is also important to realize the associated costs can be high. The account may be free; but, there may be fees associated with a transaction, especially if your bank does not own the ATM. Finally, there may be security questions. In fact, electronic identity stealing is a rapidly rising crime.

ONLINE BANKING

With a computer and appropriate software it is often possible to do most of your banking from home. With an access code you can view your account status, transfer funds, or pay bills without writing a check or going to the bank.

Still other valuable services are provided by each individual bank. You might want to investigate the special services offered by the bank where your parents do their business.

$$

Match the name of each bank service to its description.

2.35 _____ cashier's check   a. a storage place for valuable items

2.36 _____ currency exchange   b. a check that can be replaced if it is lost or stolen

2.37 _____ financial counseling   c. a check that is guaranteed by the bank itself

2.38 _____ safety deposit box   d. a service related to investments and estate planning

2.39 _____ traveler's check   e. a check that never needs to be paid for

Teacher check_____ f. a service to provide customers with money of foreign countries

                Initial   Date

REVIEW   Review the material in this section in preparation for the Self Test. This Self Test will check your mastery of this particular section as well as your knowledge of the previous section.

SELF TEST 2

(Students will need access to all tables for Sections I and II to complete Self Test 2.)

Complete the following checks. Use today's date, and sign the checks with your own signature (each check, 4 points).

2.01   Make check #1458 out to J. B. Maddox, M.D. Make it for $7.75.

CITY BANK
MAIN AND CENTRAL OFFICE
PHOENIX, ARIZONA

1458
2-631
710

PAY TO THE ORDER OF _____ $ _____

_____ DOLLARS

MEMO _____

⑆710⋯0631⑆   ⋯0631⋯9088⑈   ⑆00000775⑆

2.02   Make check #1459 to Christian Book Store, in the amount of
       $19.43.   In the memo space, write "Bibles."

```
                                                              1459
   CITY BANK                                                  2-631
   MAIN AND CENTRAL OFFICE                                     710
   PHOENIX, ARIZONA                          _____ 2 _____

   PAY
   TO THE
   ORDER OF _____ $ _____

   _____ DOLLARS


   MEMO _____          _____

   ⑈P10⋯0631⋮      ⋯0631⋯9088⋯⋮         ⋰00001943⋰
```

Enter the following figures on the checking-account record and add
or subtract them to keep the running total correct (each entry,
3 points).

2.03   a. Balance forward $1,034.27

        b. Check #5734 to Luphe's Market, for food, for $78.21

        c. Deposit of $431.80, a paycheck

        d. Check #5735 to Broadmoor Community Church, for tithe,
            in the amount of $43.18

        e. Check #5736 to Bill Baughman, for plumbing services,
            for $50.00

CHECK NO.	DATE	CHECKS ISSUED TO OR DESCRIPTION OF DEPOSIT		AMOUNT OF CHECK	AMOUNT OF DEPOSIT	BALANCE FORWARD	
		To				Check or Dep.	
		For				Bal.	
		To				Check or Dep.	
		For				Bal.	
		To				Check or Dep.	
		For				Bal.	
		To				Check or Dep.	
		For				Bal.	
		To				Check or Dep.	
		For				Bal.	
		To				Check or Dep.	
		For				Bal.	

Number correctly the five steps to be used in balancing a bank statement (each answer, 2 points).

2.04   a._____   Add to bank's record any deposits not yet credited.

        b._____   Compare the totals of your record and the bank statement.

        c._____   Subtract outstanding check total from bank's ending balance.

        d._____   Locate and add the amounts of outstanding checks.

        e._____   Subtract from your record book any charges not yet recorded.

Complete these items (each answer, 3 points).

2.05   Find the total amount and the amount of interest earned on $6,500 at 6% for 25 years.

	TOTAL AMOUNT	INTEREST AMOUNT
compounded annually	a._____	b._____
compounded semiannually	c._____	d._____
compounded quarterly	e._____	f._____

2.06   List three services of a bank other than checking accounts, savings accounts, loans, and credit cards.

        a. _____

        b. _____

        c. _____

2.07   What is Ruth Berger's age for insurance purposes on May 18, 1981, if she was born on April 3, 1930?

                                        _____

2.08   Find the premium of $30,000 worth of ordinary whole
       life insurance for a fifty-year-old man.

                              annual   a. _____

                              semiannual   b. _____

                              quarterly   c. _____

                              monthly   d. _____

Match the type of insurance to its definition (each answer, 2
points).

2.09   _____ limited-payment life   a. covers insured for life; is
                                           paid on for life

2.010 _____ bodily injury auto
                                        b. covers insured for a specific
2.011 _____ comprehensive auto   term

2.012 _____ endowment life   c. pays if insured is at fault
                                           and someone else is hurt

2.013 _____ property damage auto   d. covers insured for life; is
                                           paid on for a specific number
                                           of years

2.014 _____ medical payment auto
                                        e. provides life insurance and
2.015 _____ term life   savings

                                        f. pays if auto is stolen
2.016 _____ collision auto
                                        g. pays if insured is at fault
2.017 _____ ordinary whole life   and someone else's property
                                           is damaged

                                        h. pays if insured is at fault
                                           and insured is hurt

                                        i. pays if insured is at fault
                                           and insured's auto is damaged

75 / 93

OBJECTIVES

13. To calculate the return on shares of stocks, based on declared dividends.

14. To list several ways of disposing of an estate.

The Bible teaches us that God is the source of all good things. James 1:17 states, ". . . Every good gift and every perfect is from above, and cometh down from the Father. . . ." When God blesses us with financial riches, we should know how to handle them. This section will briefly treat investments and stocks. It will also present the importance of making provisions for one's estate after death. You probably do not have what could be called an estate now, but the day may come when you will. This section will help to prepare you for that day.

MAKING INVESTMENTS

Money can be used to make money for you. We have already mentioned savings accounts, accounts in which money earns interest. Savings accounts are very secure. Money placed in savings accounts is insured against the failure of the banking institution by the Federal Government, in most cases. Placing your money in a savings account involves very little risk.

If you wish to earn more interest with your money than you can earn in a savings account, you must invest it. Investments can be undertaken in many ways, with varying degrees of risk and profit. When the time comes that you have a large sum of money to invest, you need to seek the advice of an investment counselor whom you trust.

We shall not try to cover all of the many ramifications of investments in this LIFEPAC. However, we shall discuss investing in stocks, which are a common type of investment for profit.

When a person purchases *stock* in a company, he is in reality buying a part of the company. As a stockholder, he shares in the profits (and the losses) of the company. He is also invited to the meetings of the stockholders and allowed to express his opinion as to what the company should do. Most small stockholders do not exercise this privilege, but they may if they wish.

When a company makes a profit, it declares *dividends* to its stockholders. The dividends are divided equally among the shares of stock. Dividends are part of the return you receive on your investment when you buy stock. Another part of your return may be that if the company becomes successful, you can sell your stock for more money than you paid for it.

DEFINITIONS

Stock is a share in the ownership of a company.

A *dividend* is a share of the money earned as profits by a company and distributed to its stockholders.

Model: XYZ Company declares dividends of $50,000. Samuel Smith owns 50 shares of stock. The company has sold 25,000 total shares of stock. To find out what Sam's share of the declared dividends is, first find out how much per share is to be paid. To do this step we divide the total dividends by the number of shares. $50,000 divided by 25,000 shares is $2.00 per share. Then we multiply the amount per share by the number of shares that Sam owns: $2.00 x 50 = $100.00. Sam will receive $100.00.

Solve the following dividend problems.

3.1   Ink, Inc., has 40,000 shares of stock outstanding. The company declares dividends of $120,000.

   a. What is the dividend per share of stock? _____

   b. If I own 45 shares of stock, what is my share of the declared dividends? _____

.3.2   MS & T has 100,000 shares of stock outstanding.

   a. If it declares dividends of $50,000, what is the dividend per share? _____

   b. Marty owns 25 shares of stock in MS & T. What is his share of this declared dividend? _____

3.3   Splash Pool Corporation has 50,000 shares of stock outstanding.

   a. If it declares dividends of $37,500, what is the dividend per share of stock? _____

   b. What would be your share of the declared dividend if you owned 75 shares? _____

3.4   Sun Country Bus Lines has 80,000 shares of stock outstanding.

   a. What would the dividend per share of stock be from a dividend declaration of $109,600? _____

   b. How many shares of stock does Julie Norris hold if her share of the dividend is $6.85? _____

3.5   Alameda Tent Company has 75,000 shares of stock outstanding.

   a. What total dividend declaration would be necessary for the dividend per share to be $1.00? _____

   b. If Chuck's share of the dividend is $50.00, how many shares does he own? _____

～～～ DISPOSING OF AN ESTATE ～～～

While a Christian lives, he is responsible to God for the way he uses the material possessions that God has given him. The Bible teaches that we are only stewards; the earth and everything in it belong to God and He lets us take care of it for Him.

This responsibility for exercising good stewardship of possessions extends beyond the earthly life of a person. The responsibilities of a Christian include making sure that after his death his material possessions will continue to serve God. Especially, a Christian father and provider must arrange that his affairs are taken care of in such a way that his wife and children do not suffer financially after his death.

According to the latest figures, 70 per cent of the people who die each year in the United States die *intestate*, or without a will. A person who dies intestate leaves his property to be distributed according to the laws of the state in which he lives. These laws often do not reflect at all what the person would have wanted done with his material possessions.

DEFINITION

Intestate means without a will.

A person can dispose of his estate in one of five basic ways.

1. He can neglect to make a will, in which case the law will dispose of his estate.

2. He can put all his property into joint ownership; that is, he can provide that he and his wife own all his property jointly. In most states, this action makes his wife the sole owner upon his death. A problem arises in this case if the man and his wife die at the same time.

3. He can make a will that distributes outright all of his estate to one or several named persons or institutions.

4. He can make a will leaving his estate in *trust*.

5. He can dispose of his estate while he is still living by placing it in a *living trust* or by giving it away.

All of these options, with the exception of putting an estate in some type of trust, are fairly easy to understand. The first option, clearly, should not be chosen by any responsible adult. Each of the other options has its advantages. A person should discuss the disposal of his estate with a lawyer or trust officer as soon as he is an adult with any appreciable material possessions at all.

Now, let us look at a *trust*. Essentially, a trust is an agreement whereby a person or bank manages the estate according to the specific directions of the owner of the estate. For example, an estate might be put in trust to provide for the education of minor children. In this case, when the minor children reach a certain age, the trust would be discontinued, and the estate would be distributed according to the stated wishes of the one who established the trust.

A *living trust* is established while the owner of the property or money put in trust is still alive. The estate is managed, invested, and controlled by the trust agency or person. The profit is paid to the owner during his lifetime, and to whomever he names upon his death.

DEFINITIONS

A *trust* is an estate, or other property or money, given to a person or institution to manage.

A *living trust* is a trust established while the owner of the trust is still alive.

▮▮▮ (OPTIONAL) Complete these exercises.

3.6 Find out if your parents have wills. Find out what the provisions of these wills are. Join a class discussion about the things you find out.

3.7 Pretend you are the father (or mother) of four children, two of them still minors in school. Make a short list of the ways you would want your estate to be divided in the event of your death.

 Teacher check _____
                              Initial   Date

REVIEW Before you take this last Self Test, you may want to do one or more of these self checks.

1. _____ Read the objectives. Determine if you can do them.

2. _____ Restudy the material related to any objectives that you cannot do.

3. _____ Use the SQ3R study procedure to review the material:

   a. Scan the sections.
   b. Question yourself again (review the questions you wrote initially).
   c. Read to answer your questions.
   d. Recite the answers to yourself.
   e. Review areas you didn't understand.

4. _____ Review all activities, and Self Tests, writing a correct answer for each wrong answer.

SELF TEST 3

(Students will need access to all tables to complete Self Test 3.)

List the five ways a person can dispose of his estate (each answer, 3 points).

3.01 _____

_____

_____

3.02 _____

_____

_____

3.03 _____

_____

_____

3.04 _____

_____

_____

3.05 _____

_____

_____

Write a short paragraph discussing the reasons why a Christian should make a will (this item, 10 points).

3.06 _____

_____

_____

_____

_____

_____

_____

Find the annual premiums for the insurance policies described in each of the following problems (each answer, 3 points).

3.07 A 20-pay life insurance policy on a 34-year-old woman, with a face value of $40,000

_____

3.08 A policy for 10/20 bodily injury auto insurance for a driver in Class 1A

_____

3.09 A policy for $100-deductible collision insurance for a 3-year-old full-size car with a Class 2A driver

_____

3.010 Property damage auto insurance in the amount of $5,000 for a driver in Class 3, who had four accidents last year

_____

3.011 An endowment life insurance policy taken out by an 18-year-old-man, for $20,000

_____

3.012 A $35,000 ordinary whole-life insurance policy purchased by Abe Snyder on May 12, 1975 (Abe was born May 11, 1927)

_____

Complete these items (each answer, 3 points).

3.013 List three kinds of insurance besides life and auto.

a. _____

b. _____

c. _____

3.014   Use the following figures to find out if an error exists
        either in the bank's balance or the customer's record book.

              The ending balance on the statement is $378.19. Three
        checks are outstanding: #5104 for $30.90; #5123 for $17.50;
        and #5124 for $98.10. A deposit of $309.00 has not yet
        been credited. A service charge of $4.21 has been made.
        The balance in the record book is $544.90. Does an error
        exist?

        _____

3.015   Find the total amount and the amount of interest earned on
        $150 at 6% for 20 years.

                                          TOTAL   INTEREST
                                          AMOUNT   AMOUNT

                compounded annually   a._____   b._____

                compounded semiannually a._____   b._____

                compounded quarterly   a._____   b._____

3.016   Find the interest due to the bank on a loan of $1,000 at
        7.5% for 280 days.

        _____

3.017   Zeller, Inc., has 50,000 shares of stock outstanding.
        Zeller declares a dividend of $480,000. What is the
        dividend per share?

        _____

Number correctly the five steps to be used in balancing a bank
statement (each answer, 2 points).

3.018   a._____   Subtract from your record book any charges not yet
                  recorded.

        b._____   Locate and add the amounts of outstanding checks.

        c._____   Compare the totals of your record and the bank
                  statement.

        d._____   Subtract outstanding check total from bank's ending
                  balance.

        e._____   Add to bank's record any deposits not yet credited.

57

Before taking the LIFEPAC Test, you may want to do one or more of these self checks.

1. _____ Read the objectives. Check to see if you can do them.
2. _____ Restudy the material related to any objective that you cannot do.
3. _____ Use the SQ3R study procedure to review the material.
4. _____ Review activities, Self Tests, and LIFEPAC Glossary.
5. _____ Restudy areas of weakness indicated by the last Self Test.

GLOSSARY

annually. Once a year.

beneficiary. The survivor to whom insurance benefits are paid.

benefit. The amount paid to a survivor upon the death of a person with life insurance.

collision insurance. Automobile insurance covering damage to the automobile of the insured.

compound interest. Interest figured on the principal and on the interest already due.

comprehensive insurance. Automobile insurance covering such events as theft and vandalism; not affected by the class of the driver.

dividend. A share of the money earned as profit by a company and distributed to its stockholders.

face value. The stated amount of an insurance policy.

fire insurance. Insurance covering damages caused by fire.

homeowners' insurance. Insurance covering a loss of home or furnishings by natural disasters.

hospitalization insurance. Insurance covering the expenses of a hospital stay.

insured. The person purchasing insurance.

interest. Money paid for the use of money.

intestate. Having made no legal will. One who dies without a legal will.

liability insurance. Insurance protecting against injury to others on the insured's property.

living trust. A trust established while the owner of the trust is still alive.

medical payments insurance. Insurance covering injury to the insured from an automobile accident.

outstanding checks. Checks written but not yet returned to the bank to be subtracted from the account.

premium. The amount of money paid for insurance.

quarterly. Four times a year.

semiannually. Twice a year.

simple interest. Interest figured only on the principal.

stock. A share in the ownership of a company.

trust. An estate, or other property or money, given to a person or institution to manage.

TYPICAL ANNUAL LIFE INSURANCE PREMIUMS
FOR MALES, PER $1,000 FACE VALUE

Age	10-Year Term	Ordinary Whole Life	20-Payment Life	20-Year Endowment
18	$ 3.98	$ 9.98	$18.18	$42.01
19	3.99	10.32	18.60	42.01
20	4.00	10.67	19.03	42.01
21	4.02	11.01	19.46	42.07
22	4.06	11.34	19.89	42.15
23	4.10	11.69	20.32	42.24
24	4.15	12.05	20.78	42.34
25	4.20	12.44	21.27	42.45
26	4.29	12.86	21.79	42.56
27	4.41	13.30	22.34	42.67
28	4.54	13.77	22.91	42.79
29	4.69	14.26	23.51	42.92
30	4.87	14.78	24.12	43.05
31	5.07	15.33	24.75	43.19
32	5.29	15.90	25.40	43.33
33	5.54	16.50	26.06	43.48
34	5.81	17.13	26.76	43.64
35	6.11	17.81	27.48	43.81
36	6.43	18.52	28.23	44.00
37	6.76	19.26	28.99	44.19
38	7.12	20.04	29.79	44.40
39	7.53	20.87	30.62	44.63
40	8.00	21.75	31.50	44.87
41	8.52	22.69	32.43	45.12
42	9.08	23.69	33.41	45.39
43	9.70	24.73	34.43	45.67
44	10.38	25.82	35.46	45.98
45	11.16	26.94	36.51	46.31
46	12.02	28.09	37.55	46.65
47	12.94	29.27	38.60	46.99
48	13.95	30.50	39.68	47.37
49	15.05	31.78	40.80	47.81
50	16.25	33.14	41.98	48.34
51	17.51	34.55	43.21	48.94
52	18.83	36.00	44.48	49.60
53	20.25	37.53	45.81	50.34
54	21.85	39.17	47.21	51.20
55	23.68	40.95	48.72	52.21

Notes: (1) For semiannual premiums, use 51% of the annual rate.

(2) For quarterly premiums, use 26% of the annual rate.

(3) For monthly premiums, use 9% of the annual rate.

(4) For females, use the age of a male three years younger.

NOTE: Examples of premiums on this chart are for practice and calculation purposes. The amounts may not reflect what the student is familiar with.

AUTOMOBILE LIABILITY BASIC INSURANCE PREMIUMS

Coverage	Class 1A	Class 1B	Class 1C	Class 2A	Class 2B	Class 3
Bodily Injury (in $1.000's)						
10/20	317.80	365.40	413.40	587.00	761.00	428.40
50/100	383.60	440.70	497.80	709.30	917.90	517.60
100/300	407.50	469.90	530.92	751.88	976.96	549.70
Property Damage						
$ 5,000	61.00	69.40	79.80	113.40	163.80	81.80
$10,000	67.00	76.20	87.80	124.80	180.00	90.00
$25,000	73.20	84.80	96.80	136.00	196.60	98.20

Class 1A: No male driver under 25; car not used for business and not driven to or from work.

Class 1B: No male driver under 25; car not used for business and driven to work fewer than ten miles away.

Class 1C: No male driver under 25; car not used for business and driven to work at least ten miles away.

Class 2A: One or more male drivers under 25 who are married or not owner(s) of the car.

Class 2B: Unmarried male driver under 25 who is owner of the car.

Class 3: No male driver under 25; car used for business.

Figure 2

ANNUAL PREMIUM
FOR AUTOMOBILE MEDICAL PAYMENT

Limit	Class 1A, 1B	Class 1C, 2A, 2C, 3
$ 500	$20	$22
750	22	24
1,000	26	28
2,000	28	30
5,000	17	18

Figure 3

NOTE: Examples of premiums on this page are for practice and calculation purposes. The amounts may not reflect what the student is familiar with.

ANNUAL AUTOMOBILE COLLISION INSURANCE RATES

| Kind of Car | Age of Car | Class of Driver or Usage — Deductible: | | | | | | | |
| | | Class 1 | | Class 2A | | Class 2B | | Class 3 | |
		$ 50	$100	$ 50	$100	$ 50	$100	$ 50	$100
Compact	New	106	58	152	84	200	110	132	72
	1 or 2 years old	94	52	136	74	176	98	118	66
	3 or more years old	80	44	116	64	150	82	100	56
Full-Size	New	128	82	184	118	240	154	160	102
	1 or 2 years old	112	72	162	104	210	136	140	90
	3 or more years old	96	62	138	90	180	116	120	78
Luxury	New	238	172	342	248	448	324	298	216
	1 or 2 years old	208	150	300	216	392	282	260	188
	3 or more years old	178	130	256	188	334	244	222	162

Figure 4

ANNUAL AUTOMOBILE COMPREHENSIVE INSURANCE RATES
(Non-Deductible)

Size of Car \ Age of Car	New	1 or 2 Years Old	3 or More Years Old
Compact	$26	$22	$16
Full-Size	32	28	20
Luxury	98	84	60

Figure 5

NOTE: Examples of insurance rates on this page are for practice and calculation purposes. The amounts may not reflect what the student is familiar with.

AMOUNT OF $1 AT COMPOUND INTEREST

Number of Interest Periods	1½%	2%	3%	4%	6%	8%
1	1.0150000	1.0200000	1.0300000	1.0400000	1.0600000	1.0800000
2	1.0302250	1.0404000	1.0609000	1.0816000	1.1236000	1.1664000
3	1.0456784	1.0612080	1.0927270	1.1248640	1.1910160	1.2597120
4	1.0613636	1.0824322	1.1255088	1.1698586	1.2624770	1.3604890
5	1.0772840	1.1040808	1.1592741	1.2166529	1.3382256	1.4693281
6	1.0934433	1.1261624	1.1940523	1.2653190	1.4185191	1.5868743
7	1.0908449	1.1486857	1.2298739	1.3159318	1.5036303	1.7138243
8	1.1264926	1.1716594	1.2667701	1.3685690	1.5938481	1.8509302
9	1.1433900	1.1950926	1.3047732	1.4233118	1.6894790	1.9990046
10	1.1605408	1.2189944	1.3439164	1.4802443	1.7908477	2.1589250
11	1.1779489	1.2433743	1.3842339	1.5394541	1.8982986	2.3316390
12	1.1956182	1.2682418	1.4257609	1.6010322	2.0121965	2.5181701
13	1.2135524	1.2936066	1.4685337	1.6650735	2.1329283	2.7196237
14	1.2317557	1.3194788	1.5125897	1.7316764	2.2609040	2.9371936
15	1.2502321	1.3458683	1.5579674	1.8009435	2.3965582	3.1721691
16	1.2689856	1.3727857	1.6047064	1.8729812	2.5403517	3.4259426
17	1.2880203	1.4002414	1.6528476	1.9479005	2.6927728	3.7000181
18	1.3073406	1.4282462	1.7024331	2.0258165	2.8543392	3.9960195
19	1.3269508	1.4568112	1.7535061	2.1068492	3.0255995	4.3157011
20	1.3468550	1.4859474	1.8061112	2.1911231	3.2071355	4.6609571
25	1.4509454	1.6406060	2.0937779	2.6658363	4.2918707	6.8484752
30	1.5630802	1.8113616	2.4272625	3.2433975	5.7434912	10.0626569
40	1.8140184	2.2080397	3.2620378	4.8010206	10.2857179	21.7245215
50	2.1052424	2.6915880	4.3839060	7.1066834	18.4201543	46.9016125
60	2.4432198	3.2810308	5.8916031	10.5196274	32.9876908	101.2570637
70	2.8354563	3.9995582	7.9178219	15.4716184	59.0759302	218.6064059
80	3.2906628	4.8754392	10.6408906	23.0497991	105.7959935	471.9548343
90	3.8189485	5.9431331	14.3004671	34.1193333	189.4645112	1018.9150893
100	4.4320457	7.2446461	19.2186320	50.5049482	339.3020835	2199.7612563

Figure 8